SELFIE

THE CHANGING FACE OF SELF-PORTRAITS

Susie Brooks

WAYLAND
www.waylandbooks.co.uk

First published in Great Britain in 2016 by Wayland

Copyright © Wayland, 2016

All rights reserved.
ISBN: 978 0 7502 9964 0
10 9 8 7 6 5 4 3 2 1

Printed in China

Wayland
An imprint of
Hachette Children's Group
Part of Hodder & Stoughton
Carmelite House
50 Victoria Embankment
London EC4Y 0DZ

An Hachette UK Company
www.hachette.co.uk
www.hachettechildrens.co.uk

Editor: Elizabeth Brent
Designer: Lisa Peacock

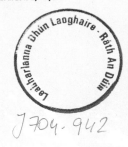

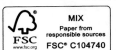

J704.942

MIX
Paper from
responsible sources
FSC® C104740
www.fsc.org

The website addresses (URLs) and QR codes included in this book were
valid at the time of going to press. However, it is possible that contents
or addresses may have changed since the publication of this book.
No responsibility for any such changes can be accepted by either the
author or the Publisher.

Picture acknowledgements:
Cover: (top) The Art Archive/National Gallery London/Eileen Tweedy,
(bottom middle) The Art Archive/Courtauld Institute London/Superstock,
(bottom) The Art Archive/Museo del Prado Madrid; p2: Ellen DeGeneres/
Twitter via Getty Images; p4: The Art Archive/Courtauld Institute
London/Superstock; p5: Fabio Lamanna/Shutterstock.com; p6: The Art
Archive/DeA Picture Library; p7: (top) The Art Archive/Egyptian Museum,
Berlin/Werner Forman Archive, (bottom) Frater Rufillus/Wikicommons;

p8: The Art Archive/National Gallery London/Eileen Tweedy; p9: The
Archive/National Gallery London/Eileen Tweedy; p10: The Art Archiv
Museo del Prado Madrid; p11: The Art Archive/Bibliothèque des Arts
Décoratifs Paris/Gianni Dagli Orti; p12: The Art Archive/Room of the
Segnature, Vatican Palace, Vatican Museum, Vatican City/Mondado
Portfolio/Electa; p13: The Art Archive/Sistine Chapel Vatican/Supers
p14: The Art Archive/Private Collection Italy/Gianni Dagli Orti; p16: T
Art Archive/Museo del Prado Madrid/Gianni Dagli Orti; p17: (left) Th
Art Archive/Royal Collection/Superstock/Fine Art Images, (right) T
Art Archive/Pinacoteca di Brera, Milan/Mondadori Portfolio/Electa;
(top) The Art Archive/DeA Picture Library/E. Lessing, (bottom) The
Archive/National Gallery London/Eileen Tweedy; p19: The Art Archiv
Galleria degli Uffizi Florence/Collection Dagli Orti; p20: The Art Arc
National Gallery London/Eileen Tweedy; p21: The Art Archive/Natio
Gallery London/Eileen Tweedy; p22: Self-Portrait, Yawning, 1783 (oi
canvas), Ducreux, Joseph (1735-1802)/J. Paul Getty Museum, Los An
USA/Bridgeman Images; p23: The Art Archive/Slovak National Gall
Bratislava/Superstock; p24: The Art Archive/Musée Fabre Montpelie
Gianni Dagli Orti; p26: Wikicommons; p27: Wikicommons; p29: The
Archive/Courtauld Institute London/Superstock; p30: The Art Arch
Private Collection/Gianni Dagli Orti, All rights reserved. DACS 2015
Self-Portrait, 1907 (oil on canvas), Picasso, Pablo (1881-1973)/Národn
Galerie, Prague, Czech Republic/Bridgeman Images. All rights rese
DACS 2015.; p33: Sergey Uryadnikov/Shutterstock.com; p35: The A
Archive/DeA Picture Library/E. Lessing. All rights reserved. DACS :
p36: The Art Archive/Museum of Modern Art Mexico/Gianni Dagli C
rights reserved. DACS 2015.; p37: The Art Archive/Gianni Dagli Ort
rights reserved. DACS 2015.; p38: Self-Portrait at the Mirror, Parmig
(Francesco Mazzola) (1503-40)/Kunsthistorisches Museum, Vienna,
Austria/Ali Meyer/Bridgeman Images; p39: The Art Archive/Thysse
Bornemisza Museum, Madrid, Spain/Mondadori Portfolio/Electa. ©
Lucian Freud Archive/Bridgeman Images; p40: The Art Archive/Priv
Collection Paris © The Estate of Francis Bacon. All rights reserved.
2015.; p43: The Art Archive/The Solomon R. Guggenheim Foundatic
Resource, NY/Solomon R. Guggenheim Museum, New York. Gift, A
and Anthony d'Offay in honor of Thomas Krens, 1992. All rights res
DACS 2015.; p44: Ellen DeGeneres/Twitter via Getty Images; p45:
FILIPPO MONTEFORTE/AFP/Getty Images; (bottom) Wikicommons

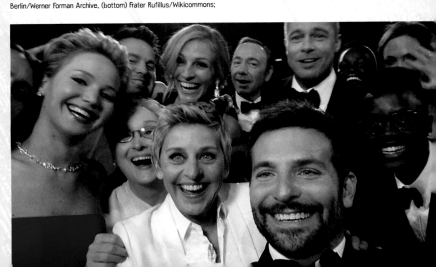

Contents

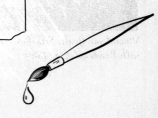

All By Your Selfie

You can probably do it with your eyes closed: point your phone camera at your face; press the shutter button and bingo — a selfie! But next time you smile/hug a celebrity and post the pic on Instagram, spare a thought for Leonardo da Vinci, Frida Kahlo, Rembrandt van Rijn, and Vincent van Gogh, among others. They never saw a smartphone, or the Internet, and most of them couldn't even tell you what a camera was. But they did all know about selfies!

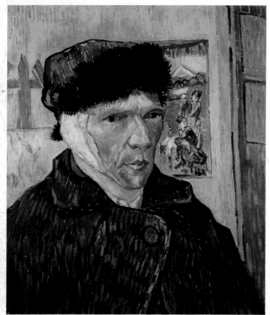

Vincent van Gogh: Self-Portrait with Bandaged Ear, 1889

Back in the old days, selfies were more commonly know self-portraits. Before photograp was invented, people who wan pictures of themselves (and co afford it) commissioned artists paint their portraits. If you wer an artist it was even easier — you just looked in the mirror and painted what you saw!

It didn't stop when photography appeared. Over the years, all kinds of artists have discovered that one of the handiest, most fascinating subjects of all is sit right there, in their very own sk

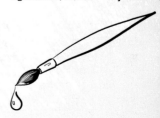

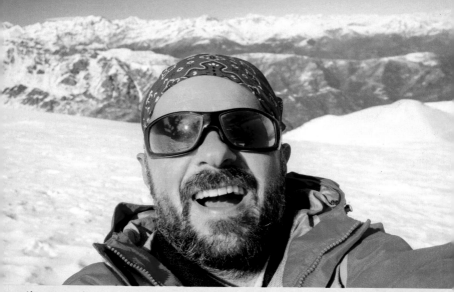

Self-Portrait of Unknown Man, 2015

Self-portraits can often tell us about the clothing of a particular time, about art materials and styles, and how old or rich or handsome the artist was or is – but most of all they let us look right inside the minds of the brilliant (and sometimes a bit bonkers) people who created them.

Take Vincent van Gogh, who cut off a piece of his ear, but still thought it would make a nice picture. Rembrandt drew, painted and etched his own reflection so many times we can see almost every stage of his life! Some modern artists have painted or sculpted their feelings through strange colours or abstract shapes without even a face to recognise.

There's a whole world of creative characters packed inside this book, all shown just as they wanted you to see them. Every selfie tells a story – so put down your mobile, switch off the webcam and read on!

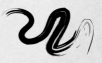

Selfies of Old

Some selfies are seriously ancient. As many as FORTY THOUSAND years ago, people were making a type of self-image by stencilling their own hands on cave walls.

Most Stone Age hand stencils seem to be left hands, suggesting the artists used their right hand to paint. They pressed a palm on the wall, then blew paint through a hollow reed or bone around the sha... Hand stencils were made by men, women and children. The oldest fou... are on the island of Sulawesi in Indonesia.

Cave paintings in Patagonia, Argentina, c.7000 BCE

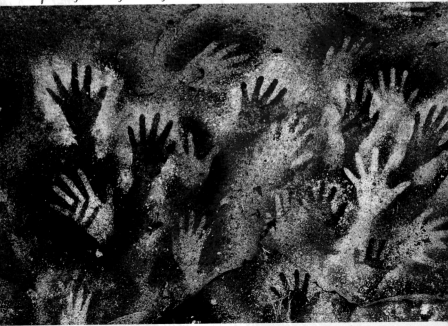

In Ancient Egypt, artists carved their self-portraits in stone. Some of the earliest examples are by Bak, chief sculptor to the Pharaoh Akhenaten. Bak was proud of his career, as we can see in this self-portrait (right). He is the one with the gigantic belly, revealing to everyone that he's rich enough to enjoy a good feast.

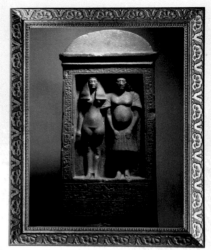

Bak, *Self-Portrait with his Wife, Taheri*, c.1353–1336 BCE

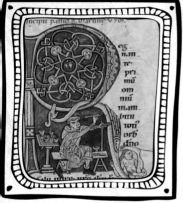

Brother Rufillus, *Self-Portrait Illuminating the Initial 'R'*, c.1170–1200

By the Middle Ages, artists in Europe were painting self-portraits into illuminated manuscripts. The printing press hadn't been invented yet, so these were written and illustrated by hand — often by monks. In the picture above, we can see Brother Rufillus of Weissenau, busy working on the initial letter of his name.

If Greek historian Plutarch is to be believed, one selfie put its maker in prison! In around 447 BCE, the sculptor Phidias made a statue of the goddess Athena for the Parthenon temple in Athens. Unfortunately he carved his face on her shield – and was locked up for being vain and disrespectful!

Now, artists have thousands of paint colours to choose from, but cave painters relied on natural pigments such as clay ochre, charcoal or burnt bones. Medieval artists also used earth, plant and animal extracts, mixed with binders such as egg white, water, honey or earwax!

Jan van Eyck

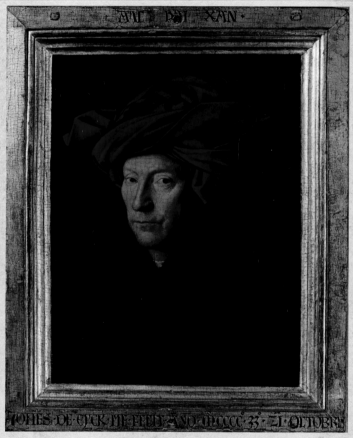

Portrait of a Man (Self-Portrait?),
1433

Born: 1390 in Belgium (though was Dutch)
Died: 1441, aged 51

Why is the man in the red turban staring straight towards us? He might be looking in a mirror, studying his own face. Most experts think that this painting is a self-portrait, because of the focussed expression and the angle of the eyes. Another clue is in van Eyck's name and motto, which he wrote in big letters on the picture's frame.

The Arnolfini Portrait, 1434

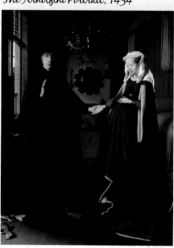

This could be the first independent self-portrait, but why did van Eyck paint it? One theory is he wanted to show off his skill — if he took the picture to his clients in person, they could see what a remarkable likeness it was. On the other hand, van Eyck was already a respected portrait artist, so perhaps he painted this as a gift, or because he had some spare time!

Van Eyck worked in oil paints, so brilliantly that people thought he invented them! Oil paints dry slowly, allowing artists to blend them and build up layers of colour. Van Eyck was a master at painting incredible, realistic detail, from the stubble on his chin to his shiny, bloodshot eyes.

This famous painting by van Eyck might also contain a selfie. One of the reflected figures in the mirror on the back wall, standing in the doorway, is thought to be the artist. He even wrote above the mirror: 'Jan van Eyck was here'!

People used to polish stone or metal (or look in water) to see their reflections. Glass mirrors were around in van Eyck's day, but they were small and usually curved. Then, in the 16th century, glass-makers in Venice, Italy, found a way to make clear, flat mirrors with a tin-mercury backing.

Albrecht Dürer

Dürer looks haughty and confident, with a stiff but elegant pose.

His clothing is expensive, extravagant and Italian in style.

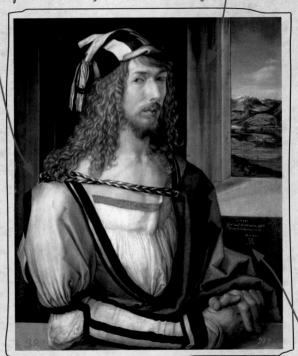

Born: 1471 in Germany
Died: 1528, aged 56

Self-Portrait, 1500

Dürer signed all his work with the monogram A

We all want to look good in a selfie — and 500 years ago it was the same. Albrecht Dürer dressed up in fancy clothes for this self-portrait, announcing to the world that he was rich and grand.

Dürer was 26 when he painted this and already a leading artist, best known for his woodcut prints. On a trip to Italy, he noticed that great artists had a higher social status than they did at home in Germany. Dürer wanted to be treated like that too!

Look at the amazing detail in Dürer's curls. He put a lot of effort into painting every strand of his hair, moustache and beard. The Italian artist, Giovanni Bellini (c.1430–1516) was so impressed with the way Dürer painted hair that he asked to see his special brushes. There was nothing special about his brushes at all!

Dürer was one of the first artists to make a series of self-portraits. His first was a drawing, done at the age of 13 when he was training as a goldsmith. Some time later he wrote proudly on the picture: 'This I have drawn from myself from the looking glass, in the year 1484, when I was still a child— Albrecht Dürer.'

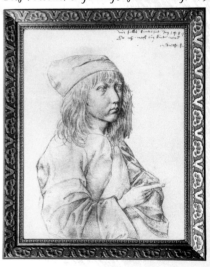

Self-Portrait, Engraving After Drawing, 1494

After Dürer's death, admirers cut locks of his hair to remember him by — you can still see some at the Academy of Fine Arts in Vienna, Austria!

Selfies in Disguise

Selfie sticks weren't around hundreds of years ago, but artists could still pictu
themselves in groups. During the Renaissance*, huge classical or religious
paintings were all the rage — and artists were their own handiest models.

The School of Athens, 150

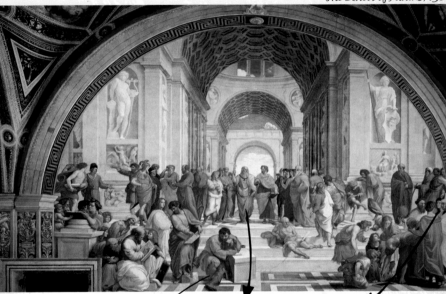

Michelangelo Leonardo da Vinci Raphael

Raphael
Born: 1483 in Ital
Died: 1520, aged 3

In 1508, Italian painter Raphael was commissioned
to decorate several rooms at the Vatican in Rome.
One of them was the Pope's library, where he began
The School of Athens in 1509. It's a fresco, which
means it is painted directly onto wet plaster on
the wall. The scene is set in Ancient Greece and
shows a range of great thinkers, from writers and
philosophers to scientists and mathematicians.

* This was a period of great
creativity in Europe, from th
14th–16th centuries. Artists
revived ideas from classical
antiquity – in other words,
Ancient Greece and Rome.

Raphael is standing with the astronomers Ptolemy and Zoroaster in this painting, who are both holding globes. Several other figures are modelled on artists that Raphael knew – including his two greatest rivals. The philosopher Plato was the face of Leonardo da Vinci (see pp14–15), while Heraclitus is Michelangelo in disguise.

While Raphael was busy at the Vatican, Michelangelo was also there, decorating the ceiling of the Sistine Chapel, where he later painted a wall with a scene called *The Last Judgement*. In this gigantic fresco, Michelangelo included his own self-portrait – on the crumpled, flayed skin of St Bartholomew. It's about as ghoulish as a selfie can be.

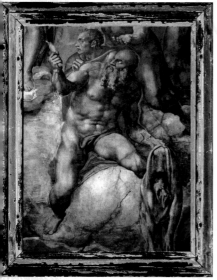

Saint Bartholomew with his Flayed Skin (detail from *The Last Judgement*), 1536–41

Born: 1475 in Italy
Died: 1564, aged 88

Some other Renaissance selfies in disguise ...

Piero della Francesca – as a sleeping soldier in *The Resurrection*, c.1460

Sandro Botticelli – as a bystander in *Adoration of the Magi*, 1475–76

Paolo Veronese – as a violinist in *The Marriage at Cana*, 1562

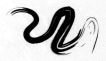

Leonardo da Vinci

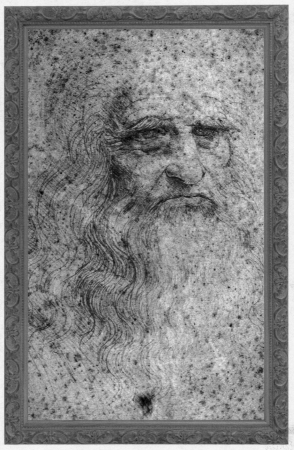

Portrait of a Man in
Red Chalk, 1512

**Born: 1452 in Italy
Died: 1519, aged 67**

With all the photos and websites around today, we can usually find out what someone looks like. But how do we recognise people from the past? Sometimes it's hard to know for sure if a painting or drawing is actually who we think it is — and that is the case with this picture.

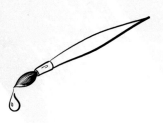

Most people agree that this drawing is by Leonardo da Vinci. It dates to his lifetime and shows the delicate lines and shading that he was famous for. Experts can tell that it was drawn with a left hand — Leonardo was left-handed — and people who wrote about him described his striking looks, long hair and flowing beard. There are portraits thought to be of him that fit this description too.

However, the date of this drawing would make Leonardo about 60, but he looks a lot older! Some people believe that he deliberately drew himself as a wise, elderly man. Others suggest that this might be his father or uncle, who both lived until they were 80.

Leonardo da Vinci was a great painter, sculptor, scientist, inventor and an all-round genius. He filled sketchbooks with designs for flying machines, musical instruments and other devices that were way ahead of his time. His studies of the human body are extraordinarily detailed, down to the tiniest veins and bones — he learned by cutting up corpses and copying them.

Leonardo wrote in mirror writing, from right to left across the page. Because he was left-handed, some people say this was to stop him smudging the ink. Others believe it was a type of code, hiding his ideas from nosy readers, or competitors.

The Artist at Work

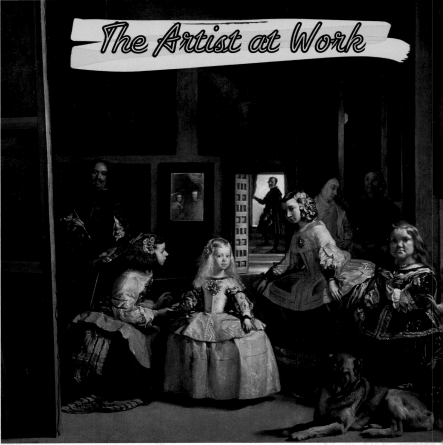

Las Meninas, 1656

Born: 1599 in Spa
Died: 1660, aged

It's easy to spot the artist in this picture – he's the one holding the brush and palette! Velázquez was a court painter for the Spanish royal family, but what is he painting here? We can only guess what's on the canvas in front of him.

There is a clue at the back of the picture. Can see a mirror on the wall? It shows the reflectio of two people who must be facing Velázquez, perhaps posing for their portraits to be painted Our eye is drawn towards them by the shapes the other figures, and by the triangle of light in scene. Who are they? The king and queen!

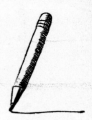

Nearly everyone in the painting is looking towards the royal couple. In the centre is the five-year-old princess, being fussed over by her meninas, or ladies-in-waiting. Velázquez is hovering in the shadows, but the enormous canvas he is painting stands out and reminds us of his importance. The artist had his own rooms in the royal palace, and he set this one up as a studio where the king would often watch him work.

Many other famous artists have painted self-portraits that show the tools of their trade. Here are just a few ...

Pieter Brueghel the Elder *The Painter and the Buyer*, 1565
Jan Vermeer *The Artist's Studio*, 1665–68
Joshua Reynolds *Self-Portrait*, 1747–48
Paul Gauguin *Self-Portrait with Palette*, c1883/84
Paul Cézanne *Self-Portrait with Palette*, 1885–87

Self-Portrait as the Allegory of Painting, 1638-39

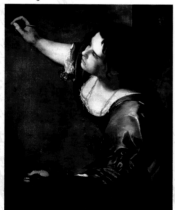

Self-Portrait, 1906

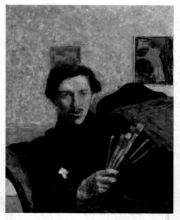

Artemisia Gentileschi
Born: 1593 in Italy
Died: c1652, aged c59

Umberto Boccioni
Born: 1882 in Italy
Died: 1916, aged 33

Rembrandt van Rijn

Self-Portr
the Age o

Rembrandt was the biggest selfie maker of his time, creating nearly 100 self-portraits, that spanned 40 years of his life. They track his changing appearance, as well as his developing painting style.

Rembrandt trained as a painter in his teens, and quickly became a massive success. Many important people in his home country, the Netherlands, commissioned him to paint. But later he went bankrupt, and suffered from the death of his wife, son and other loved ones. It helps to explain the emotion that we see in his final self-portrait (right).

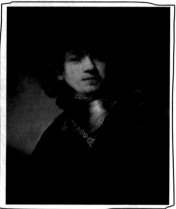

Self-Portrait as a Young Man, 1634

Rembrandt pictured himself in all sorts of poses, outfits and moods. As a young man, he often appeared in fine clothing, perhaps in the style of the rich people whose portraits he painted. Sometimes his scenes were theatrical, like this one below at the age of 29 with his wife Saskia sitting on his knee.

By the end of his life, Rembrandt was an expert at capturing character. He stripped away all the fancy dress and showed us simply Rembrandt the person. In his last self-portrait aged 63, he seems sad yet calm and dignified. We see him inside and out, with every lump, sag and wrinkle on display.

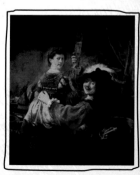

Self-Portrait with Saskia, 1636

Born: 1606 in the Netherlands
Died: 1669, aged 63

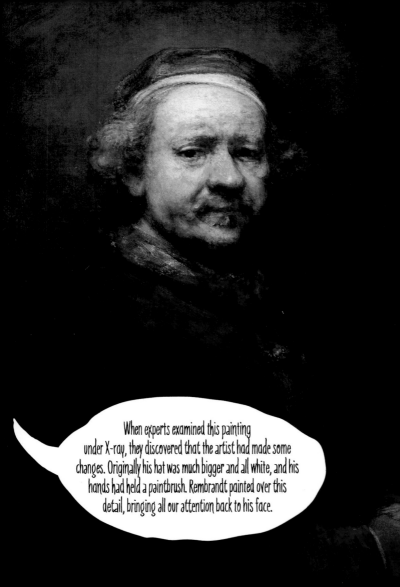

Elizabeth Vigée Le Brun

This lady looks pretty in her straw hat and pink dress. She has a gentle smile and a friendly and welcoming gaze. Vigée Le Brun wanted people to like her in this selfie — and they did.

The straw hat self-portrait was an instant hit for Vigée Le Brun – she even made copies for her admirers. It made her such a name that she was admitted to the French Royal Academy of Art. This was a great achievement, as only four women were allowed to be members at the time.

In the 18th century, female artists had to work hard to be taken seriously. Traditionally, painting was something that women did mostly as a hobby. Vigée Le Brun was extremely talented and she also sold her skills well. Self-portraits like this one were a way to attract attention and win people's hearts

Born: 1755 in France
Died: 1842, aged 86

Self-Portrait in a Straw Hat, 1782

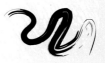

Elizabeth looks natural and relaxed in the painting. She seems comfortable with her palette and brushes, but they aren't the focus of the scene.

For people in the art world, there was something familiar about this work — it was modelled on a portrait by Peter Paul Rubens, done more than a hundred years before. Vigée Le Brun was a big fan of Rubens, so she set herself a challenge to paint in his famous style.

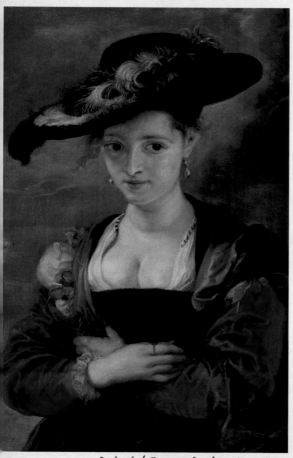

Vigée Le Brun made a living from her portraits from an early age. As her reputation grew, she caught the eye of many wealthy people, including the French queen, Marie Antoinette. Vigée Le Brun painted her more than 20 times, and made a selfie showing herself working on a portrait of the queen. When the film *Marie Antoinette* was made in 2006, Vigée Le Brun was featured in it!

Portrait of Susanna Lunden, 1622-1625

Peter Paul Rubens
Born: 1577 in Germany
Died: 1640, aged 62

Pulling Faces

These days, funny faces in selfies are nothing unusual, but in the 1700s people tended to be more straight-faced. Most self-portraits avoided any strong feeling of being happy, cross or tired. It was different for the artists on these pages, though!

Joseph Ducreux found traditional portraiture too prim and proper. Instead, he tried to capture the personalities of everyone he painted. In this self-portrait, he caught himself in the middle of a yawn. There's nothing shy or self-conscious about it — he pushes out his belly and opens his mouth wide, in a way that makes us want to yawn too.

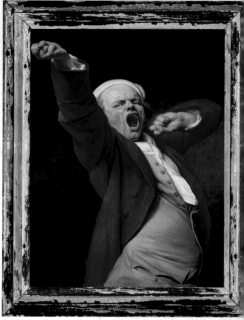

Self-Portrait, Yawning, 1783

Joseph Ducrei
Born: 1735 in Franc
Died: 1802, aged 6

Ducreux painted many other funny and expressive portraits. Today, more than 200 years after his death, his selfies are all over the Internet! Ducreux has at least two Twitter feeds and a long-running meme, where people caption his pictures with jokey, old-fashioned hip-hop lyrics.

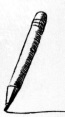

The sculptor Franz Xaver Messerschmidt pinched himself in front of a mirror to record his changing expressions! He turned his gruesome grimaces into 64 'character heads', made from stone, wood or metal. Some reports say that Messerschmidt, who was growing increasingly eccentric, made the heads to scare away ghosts and spirits that tormented him at night.

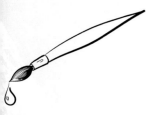

Ten years after Messerschmidt's death, there was an exhibition of the heads in Vienna, Austria, where he had once lived. The organisers gave the heads descriptive titles, including *Just Rescued from Drowning* and *Childish Weeping*! This one, *The Big Secret*, shows the face you might pull if you've just heard a secret, or are trying very hard to keep one.

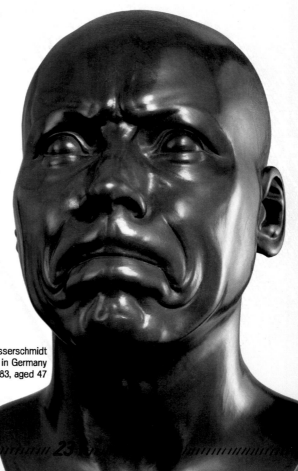

Franz Xaver Messerschmidt
Born: 1736 in Germany
Died: 1783, aged 47

The Big Secret, 1770–1783

Gustave Courbet

The painter of this selfie called himself 'the proudest and most arrogant man in France'! Can you tell which of these three figures is him? There are clues in the things he is carrying – and also in the way he has arranged the scene.

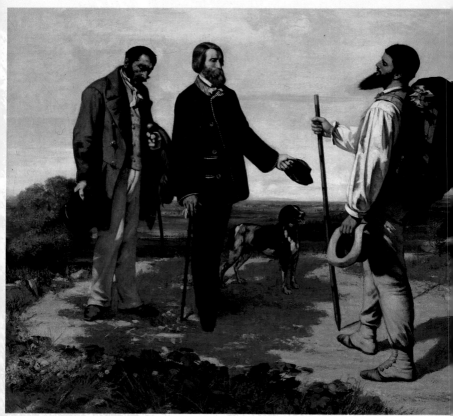

The Meeting, or Hello Mr Courbet, 1854

Born: 1819 in France
Died: 1877, aged 58

Who is the most prominent person? It's the man on the right, with a pointy beard. He is the artist, Gustave Courbet. On his back he carries an easel and a box of paints, with a canvas rolled on the top. He is standing in full sunlight, while the other two men are under the shadow of a tree.

So who are the other two figures? The man in green is Alfred Bruyas — a supporter of Courbet's work. Next to him is his servant, Calas. All three men have taken off their hats, but while Calas bows and Bruyas lowers his eyes, Courbet tips his head back confidently. He seems to be the one with the upper hand. Even the dog is standing to attention, looking up as if listening to Courbet!

Critics at the time called this a boastful painting. They laughed at the way Courbet had made such a pompous picture out of an ordinary meeting. People were used to seeing characters from the Bible, myths or history in storytelling paintings like this. Courbet was lifting an everyday experience to a new, more important level!

Courbet may have shocked people with his attitude, but he helped to set a new trend in painting. He said he wanted to show scenes of his time that he knew and understood. He painted workers in fields and peasants at a funeral. Instead of dressing things up, he showed the truth of everyday life. His style became known as Realism.

Courbet painted other attention-grabbing self-portraits — he said they told the story of his changing states of mind. In one we see him up-close, clutching his head and looking terrified. In another he lies heroic and wounded with a bullet through his heart.

The First Photos

When the first fixed photograph, or daguerrotype, was released, people were amazed, excited and even afraid! This extraordinary invention took a while to reach ordinary households, but when it did the snapshot selfie took off.

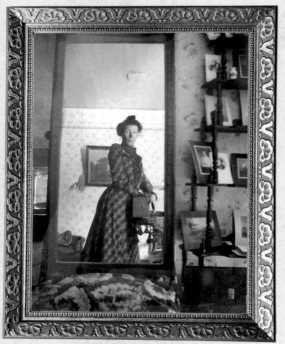

Self-Portrait of an Unidentified Lady, 1900

The daguerrotype was unveiled in 1839, by the Frenchman Louis Daguerre. It involved a simple box camera that produced a picture on a light-sensitive metal plate. People soon dreamed up variations on this idea, and about 50 years later the first camera using film went on sale. The 'Kodak' was small and easy to use, and people could take 100 pictures before sending it back to the factory for processing.

In 1900, a whole new world was opened up by the Kodak Brownie — a cheap and popular portable camera. Now anyone could take a selfie! Like this Edwardian lady, they would usually pose in front of a mirror and prop the camera on a table to keep it steady. The viewfinder was on top of the box, so the trick was to hold it at waist height and look down to compose the shot.

The Grand Duchess Anastasia Nikolaevna of Russia took one of the first teen selfies with a Kodak Brownie. She sent it to a friend, saying that it was hard to take because her hands were shaking! The Brownie was marketed at children and young people — there was even a Brownie Camera Club, offering prizes for the best pictures.

The word photography means 'drawing with light', and in the 19th century it wasn't a new idea. It developed from the camera obscura, a device that had been around since ancient times. The camera obscura projected an image onto a surface, but to keep it you had to draw over it. The image came out upside-down, until mirrors and lenses were used to correct this.

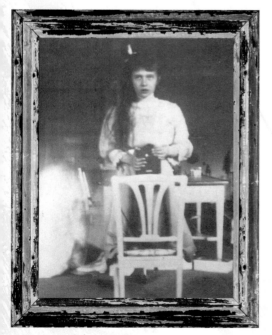

Anastasia Nikolaevna, 1914

The invention of photography had a big impact on art, especially portrait painting. There was now a quicker and cheaper way to get a picture of a person. Some artists resented the competition, while others used photographs to help their work. Painting became more experimental, moving beyond just portraying a realistic likeness.

Vincent van Gogh

You might take a selfie when something unusual happens to you. Van Gogh made this one after he cut a piece from his ear following an argument with his friend and fellow artist, Gauguin.

Can you see the bandage on the side of van Gogh's head? The unlucky ear was actually the left one, but he was looking in a mirror when he painted this. Rather than hiding his injury, he made it the focus of the picture. His face looks as if he's lost in thought.

Why is van Gogh wearing a hat and coat? Perhaps there's a draught coming in. It was wintertime, and the house in France where he lived wouldn't have had central heating. Van Gogh was poor and often spent his money on paint instead of food.

Van Gogh made more than 850 paintings in just 10 years, but he managed to sell only one in his lifetime. Now he's one of the most famous artists in history and collectors pay millions for his work!

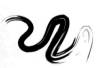

Notice how van Gogh used big, thick brushstrokes. They bring the different textures of his clothes, fur cap, bandage and bony face. Sometimes he squeezed paint straight from the tube onto the canvas, and it would take weeks and weeks to dry! Behind artist we can see a Japanese print. Van Gogh was fascinated by Japanese art. He loved its bold outlines, flat colours and shape and did his best to use them in his own work.

When he painted this selfie, van Gogh was mentally ill. After cutting the chunk off his ear, he gave it to a woman as a 'gift'. He was taken into hospital and a few months later checked into an asylum. Although he continued to paint, he was unable to recover and shot himself the following year.

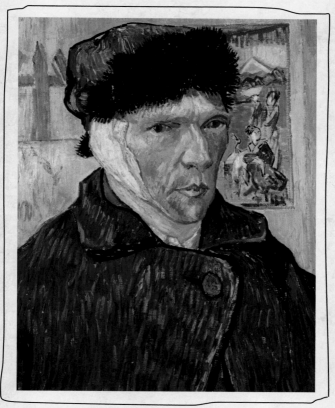

*Self-Portrait with
Bandaged Ear, 1889*

Born: 1853 in Netherlands
Died: 1890, aged 37

James Ensor

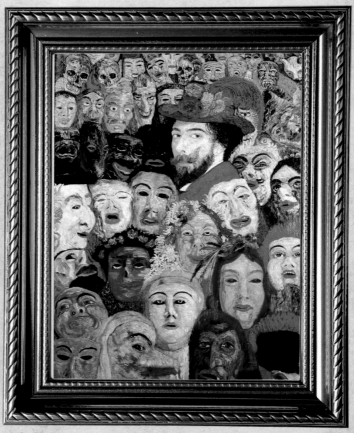

Self-Portrait Surrounded
by Masks, 1899

Born: 1860 in Belgium
Died: 1949, aged 89

There's something spooky about this selfie, staring out from a sea of masks. What is James Ensor doing here, dressed in a lady's hat? Is he trapped among the masks or is he controlling them? Is the scene real, or imagined?

Masks were a popular theme with Ensor — he loved visiting puppet theatres and reading fantasy stories. He painted masks and skeletons over and over again, and many people criticised his work. That was fine by Ensor, who wrote to a friend: 'I liked these masks, because they offended the public who had given me such a poor reception.'

Look at the faces on the masks. They are brightly painted, like clowns. Some stare, some grin and others gawp with open mouths. Are they teasing Ensor or are they his friends? It's hard to tell.

Why the feathered hat? Again we can't be certain, though costume was nothing new in the world of self-portraits. It reminds us of the hat worn by Vigée Le Brun (see pp20–21) and also the way Rembrandt (pp18–19) dressed up. Ensor painted himself in a similar hat over 10 years before, but it was green with coloured flowers.

Ensor painted 112 self-portraits. Even so, he declared, 'I've never managed to capture the resemblance.' He put himself in some strange and sometimes comical disguises — in one picture, his severed head is on a platter, being served to a table of critics!

Ensor rarely left his birthplace of Ostend in Belgium. He worked in a studio above his parents' shop. Although it took people a while to accept his unusual paintings, he became a respected artist in his time. He also helped to influence the art of the future, especially Expressionism (see p34) and Surrealism.

Pablo Picasso

This face seems quite ungainly with its thick lines, scribbled colours and jagged shapes. It looks almost like a mask, carved roughly out of wood. That tells us something about Picasso's inspiration – he had just discovered African sculpture, including tribal masks!

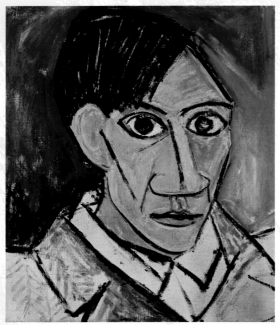

Self-Portrait, 1907

Born: 1881 in Spain
Died: 1973, aged 91

Picasso was a gifted artist, but he deliberately simplified his features here. His eyes are wide, flat, almond shapes and his nose and cheekbones are shown by minimal lines. Picasso used chunky brushstrokes and didn't try to recreate the softness or texture of skin, clothes or hair.

~~~~~~~~~~~~~~~~~~~~

At this stage in his career, Picasso was on the verge of developing a new art movement (though he may not have known it yet). The movement became known as Cubism, and was a way of representing the world as a jumble of geometric shapes.

Cubist artists blended different viewpoints, so parts of a picture look face-on, others from above and others from the left or right. In the painting on p32, the ear is seen from the side and the eyes from the front.

Picasso loved African art. He discovered it in museums in Paris where he worked, and built up a huge collection of masks, such as this one, and sculptures. They inspired him for much of his life, but especially between the years of 1907 and 1909, which became known as his 'African Period'.

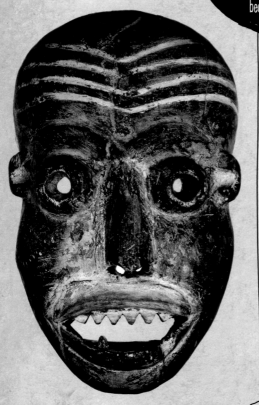

African Tribal Mask, date unknown

During his career, Picasso experimented with many different art styles and his self-portraits are really varied. Some are realistic, some are spooky, some are serious and others are funny. He drew himself as a monkey, and another time cut out a photo of his eyes and stuck them to a sketch of an owl! Picasso loved animals and kept a lot of pets, including a sausage dog called Lump.

Oscar Kokoschka

It's hard to feel happy when you look at this painting – it seems uncomfortable and distressing. The man looks sad and anxious, with his down-turned lips and a hand raised to his face. Kokoschka was excellent at painting powerful emotion.

A few years before Kokoschka made this self-portrait, the love of his life had left him and he volunteered to fight in the First World War. He was shot in the head, stabbed in the chest, and later diagnosed with shell shock (a mental illness).

When Kokoschka's girlfriend left him, he missed her so much that he had a life-size doll made of her! He used this as a model to draw and paint from in his studio.

In this painting, Kokoschka looks over his shoulder in an awkward pose and his hand touches his lips nervously. The paint is thick, slapped on with heavy brushstrokes, and there are lots of blues, greys and greens, which are cool colours. The greenish yellow of Kokoschka's face makes him look unwell.

Kokoschka's painting style was known as Expressionism – because it expressed strong feelings. It was an idea that grew up in Germany at the turn of the 20th century. Expressionist artists wanted to show what was on the inside, rather than how things looked. They exaggerated shapes and colours, and painted with big, agitated brushstrokes.

Expressionist paintings weren't all sad – some were filled with warm, cheerful colours such as reds, oranges and yellows. One group of artists used such bright and wacky colours that they were nicknamed the Fauves, or 'wild beasts'.

Self-Portrait, One Hand Touching the Face, 19

Born: 1886 in Austr
Died: 1980, aged

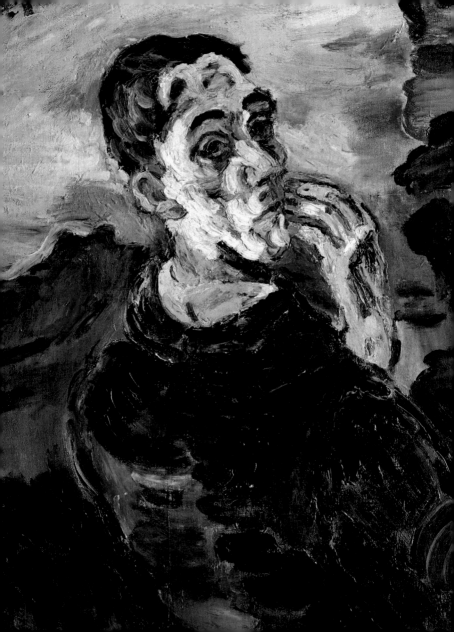

Ⓞne woman sits with a bleeding heart, while her identical twin holds her hand. In fact these are both the same person – Frida Kahlo. She was recently divorced from Diego Rivera, the artist who painted the scene on p37.

The Two Fridas, 1939

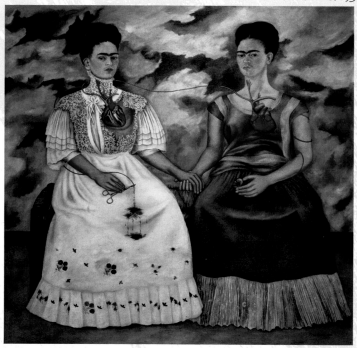

The Frida on the right is holding a portrait of Diego. A vein runs all the way from this picture, through both Fridas' hearts, to where it drips on her white dress. Although the Frida on the left is hurt, she looks calm and strengthened by the figure next to her. They don't seem to notice the storm brewing behind.

Frida Kahlo
Born: 1907 in Mexico
Died: 1954, aged 47

Kahlo was badly affected by childhood polio and injuries from a bus crash at the age of 18. To hide her impediments, she designed her own clothing with colourful skirts and supportive corsets. She suffered pain all her life, and expressed this in her work — especially self-portraits like this one.

Dream of a Sunday Afternoon in Alameda Park (detail), 1947

Kahlo took up painting while she was recovering in hospital after her accident. She had to wear full body casts, which she decorated brightly with paints. When her lower leg was amputated, she designed her own prosthetic one, dressed in a fancy red boot with a bell on it!

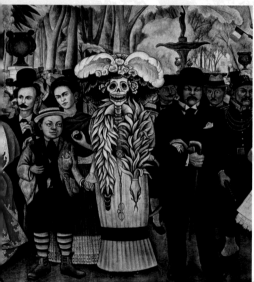

Diego Rivera included himself and Frida in a gigantic wall painting showing scenes from the history of Mexico. Of course he was grown-up at the time, but here he's a boy with a frog and snake in his pockets! Frida is right behind him, holding a Yin and Yang symbol, representing the differences between her and Diego.

Diego Rivera
Born: 1886 in Mexico
Died: 1957, aged 70

Kahlo and Rivera couldn't make up their minds about each other — they got married, divorced, then married again! When Kahlo died, Rivera ordered all her clothes be locked away until 15 years after he died too. They were rediscovered only in 2004.

Weird Reflections

What happens if you take a selfie from up high or down low? You might find you look out of shape. Lucian Freud painted this self-portrait (right) using a mirror that was flat on the floor. It's hard to make sense of the picture at first.

Notice the edge of the mirror at the bottom of the painting. Freud is looming over it with his eyes peering down towards his feet. The grey area around him is the ceiling, not a wall — you can see the round shapes of two hanging lights, as if we're looking up at them from underneath.

Looking at the painting makes us feel a bit off-balance. Freud swirled in the background using a palette knife (like a narrow metal spatula). His face is lit up, looking strained as he squints downwards. And what about the children? They seem tiny compared to the giant man next to them.

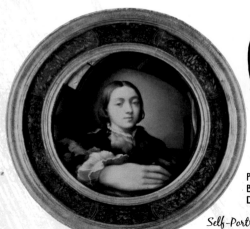

Many artists have played with weird reflections. One of the first was Parmigianino, who painted his reflection in a curved mirror, on a curved wooden panel, in 1524 when he was 21!

Parmigianino
Born: 1503 in Italy
Died: 1540, aged 37

Self-Portrait in a Convex Mirror, 1524

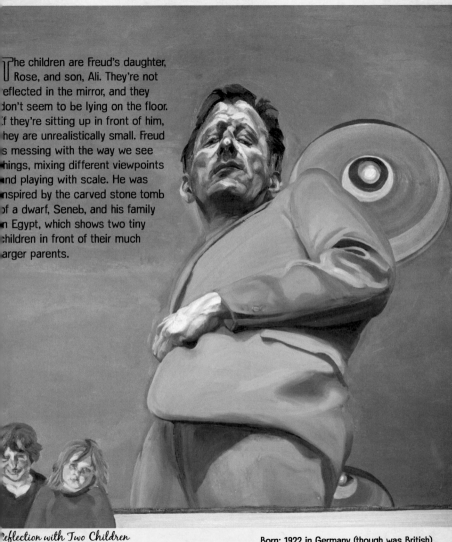

The children are Freud's daughter, Rose, and son, Ali. They're not reflected in the mirror, and they don't seem to be lying on the floor. If they're sitting up in front of him, they are unrealistically small. Freud is messing with the way we see things, mixing different viewpoints and playing with scale. He was inspired by the carved stone tomb of a dwarf, Seneb, and his family in Egypt, which shows two tiny children in front of their much larger parents.

*Reflection with Two Children
(Self-Portrait), 1965*

Born: 1922 in Germany (though was British)
Died: 2011, aged 88

Francis Bacon

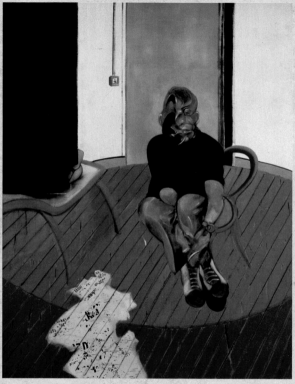

Self-Portrait, 1973

Born: 1909 in Ireland
Died: 1992, aged 82

It would be tricky to recognise this man from his face – it's all blurred and twisted out of shape! Francis Bacon didn't copy exactly what he saw in the mirror, but he had such a distinctive style of painting that we can tell straight away it is him.

Bacon liked to distort things without hiding them altogether. This figure isn't completely abstract — we can see an arm, knees and two clearly painted feet, and his face is partly visible. A lot of the background makes sense too, with the familiar shape of a chair, a door and a light switch. Bacon has painted diagonal floorboards and the oval beam from a light, to show there is space in the room. But other parts of the picture are puzzling.

Bacon largely taught himself to paint, and he didn't only use brushes. Sometimes he threw paint at the canvas, smudged it with a rag or used his fingers. If he felt like it, he mixed sand or dirt with the paint to create texture, or blended oil paints with pastels for different effects.

Like the Expressionists (see p34), Bacon chose to look at himself from the inside. He had quite a gloomy outlook on life and his self-portraits are often haunting, showing him as a lonely figure with a ghostly or monster-like head. He painted other people in a similar way, including his friend and rival Lucian Freud (p39).

Bacon worked in a famously messy studio, exploding with paint pots and colours that he tested on the walls. After his death, it was moved (walls and all) to a museum in Dublin, Ireland. There were 7,000 items in that studio! Experts took photos and made drawings and maps so that they could reconstruct it perfectly, piece by piece.

In 2013, a triple portrait of Lucian Freud by Francis Bacon sold at auction for US$142 million - a record-busting price at the time!

Andy Warhol

Imagine this green face at its actual size — more than 10 times the size of this be
It would make quite an impact hanging on a wall and Warhol was all about IMPAC

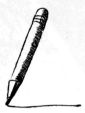

Lots of things are striking about this picture. Fo
a start, Warhol used only two colours. Green
is a peculiar choice for a face, but it glows out
against the black. Warhol's body is missing, so hi
head floats in space and his hair shoots out with
a life of its own — it is actually his trademark wig

It seems as if the artist is showing off here, as if he's flashing
his face in neon lights. Warhol loved fame and celebrity, brand
names and advertising. Anything that was eye-catching and
modern, he was ready to turn into art. His obsession with
popular culture gave his style the name 'Pop Art.'

Warhol often made multiple images,
repeating the same face in one artwork. He even created
a self-portrait wallpaper! His studio was nicknamed 'The
Factory' because of all the prints and paintings it
churned out.

Warhol created this selfie in different colours too — red, pink, blue, white and
even a camouflage pattern. He used a method called silkscreen printing,
which involved pushing ink through a type of stencil. Warhol liked the fact
that he could reproduce images, just as the images on billboards and
packaging were reproduced. He wasn't bothered about the personal touch,
saying: 'I think somebody should be able to do all my paintings for me.'

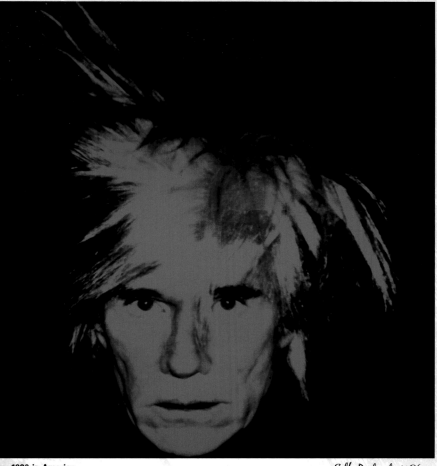

rn: 1928 in America
ed: 1987, aged 58

Self-Portrait, 1986

Warhol died the year after he made this selfie, but by then he was a celebrity himself. He had been an artist, filmmaker, photographer, writer and even a rock band manager! Warhol said that in the future everyone would be famous for 15 minutes, but his fame has lasted far longer than that. Nowadays it's easy to find a computer program that will turn your photo into a Warhol-style artwork.

Selfies Today

Selfies today are everywhere! With digital cameras and smartphones, anyone can snap themselves in an instant and share the picture with their friends or the world. Celebrities are doing it. Politicians are doing it. Even animals are doing it (sort of)! Will the selfie craze ever end?

2013 was the year that '#selfie' took off. More than 17 million people were posting a selfie on social media every week. In 2014, the word 'selfie' made it into the Oxford Dictionary and was approved for the board game Scrabble! Technologies such as front-facing cameras, selfie sticks and hand-gesture sensors have made selfie-snapping easier than ever before.

Perhaps the most famous selfie ever was taken at the Oscars in 2014, showing a gaggle of glamorous stars. Within 24 hours it was retweeted 2.8 million times!

Oscar selfie, 2014

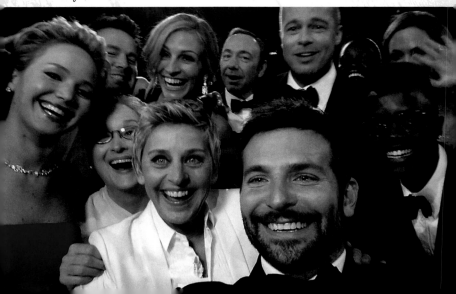

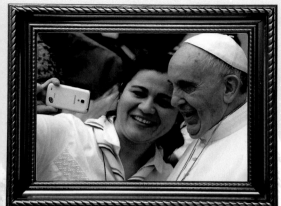

Pope Francis, 2014

In 2013, Pope Francis went viral in the first 'Papal selfie', taken with young fans at the Vatican.

This cheeky monkey in Indonesia ran off with a wildlife photographer's camera and took several crystal-clear selfies! Whether she meant to do it or not, we're not sure …

Modern artists have had some wacky ideas to capture their own image in ways that a camera can't. For example, the Bahamas-born Janine Antoni made a series of selfie sculptures out of chocolate and soap, then 'resculpted' them by licking the chocolate and bathing with the soap!

Self-Portrait of a female Celebes crested macaque, 2011

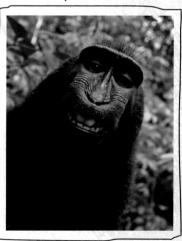

When you post a selfie, you're displaying a view of yourself that you want other people to see. When artists make self-portraits, it's the same! So next time you pose, remember you have something in common with every famous face in this book!

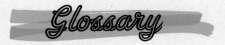

Glossary

abstract not showing the actual appearance of an object, place or living thing. Abstract art often focuses on simplified lines, shapes, colours or use of space.

auction a sale where people bid for items and the person offering the highest bid wins

camera obscura a darkened box with a hole in one side, which projects an image of something outside the box onto a surface inside

canvas a strong type of fabric that can be stretched across a frame for artists to paint on

charcoal a black substance, produced by heating wood, bone or other natural materials without any oxygen present. Artists can use charcoal to draw with.

classical relating to Ancient Greek or Roman art, literature or culture

commission to pay someone to produce something, such as a portrait or other painting

Cubism an art style (1907–1920s) in which artists made images using geometric shapes and multiple viewpoints

daguerrotype an early type of photograph, produced on a highly polished, silver-treated sheet of copper

easel a wooden stand that supports an artist's canvas or drawing board

etch to engrave a design onto glass, stone or metal, using an acid to cut into the lines. A print can then be made by spreading ink over the design and pressing it onto paper.

Expressionism an art style (1905–1920s) that was about feelings and emotions, often shown through distorted shapes or colours

grimace a twisted expression on a person's face, often showing disgust, pain or strange amusement

illuminated manuscript a book or other text that includes decorative initials, borders and miniature illustrations

illustrate to create pictures for a book or other piece of writing

lens a piece of glass with curved sides, used in cameras to focus light

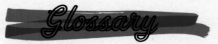

Glossary

monogram two or more letters, usually initials, woven into a design as a type of signature

mural a painting made directly onto a wall. When a mural is painted on fresh, wet plaster, this is called a fresco.

ochre an earthy, brownish-yellow pigment

oil paint a thick type of paint made by mixing powdered pigments with an oil such as linseed

palette a board that an artist mixes paint on

pastel a type of soft crayon

pigment the natural colouring found in minerals, plants and animal matter. Nowadays, synthetic pigments are often used to make paints.

Pop Art an art style (mid-1950s–1960s) that celebrated the bold, bright images of advertising, cartoon strips and popular culture

portrait an artwork that shows an image of a particular person

Renaissance a period in European history (1300s–1500s) when there were great developments in art and culture, based on the ideas of Ancient Greece and Rome

sculpt to create a 3D artwork, or sculpture. Someone who sculpts is called a sculptor.

silkscreen printing making a print by dragging ink over a stencil marked onto a silk screen. The ink goes through tiny holes in the silk that aren't covered by the stencil.

sketch a rough or unfinished drawing or painting, often done in preparation for a finished work

studio an artist's workplace

Surrealism an art style (1924–1940s) that explored the world of dreams, the imagination and the 'non-thinking' mind. Surrealist works often show familiar things, but in unexpected ways.

texture the feel of a surface, such as rough hair or smooth glass

woodcut print a print made by carving an image into a block of wood, spreading ink over it then pressing it onto paper

Index